50 Flavors of Home Recipes

By: Kelly Johnson

Table of Contents

- Classic Meatloaf
- Chicken and Dumplings
- Beef Stew
- Spaghetti and Meatballs
- Macaroni and Cheese
- Chicken Pot Pie
- Roast Chicken with Potatoes
- Baked Ziti
- Shepherd's Pie
- Sloppy Joes
- Grilled Cheese and Tomato Soup
- Chicken Alfredo
- Pulled Pork Sandwiches
- Beef Chili
- Tuna Casserole
- Baked Ham with Brown Sugar Glaze
- Sweet and Sour Meatballs
- Chicken Fried Steak
- Stir-Fried Vegetables with Rice

- Meatball Sub
- Chicken Parmesan
- Beef Tacos
- Homemade Pizza
- Eggplant Parmesan
- Fried Chicken
- BBQ Ribs
- Beef and Broccoli Stir Fry
- Spaghetti Carbonara
- Shrimp Scampi
- Grilled Hamburgers
- Potato Salad
- Biscuits and Gravy
- Fettuccine Alfredo
- Stuffed Bell Peppers
- Chicken Fajitas
- Grilled Salmon
- Beef Burritos
- Tacos al Pastor
- Chicken Quesadillas
- Fish Tacos

- Meatloaf Sandwich
- Clam Chowder
- Roasted Vegetable Soup
- Pulled Chicken Tacos
- Grilled Shrimp Skewers
- Caesar Salad with Grilled Chicken
- Baked Chicken Drumsticks
- Shepherd's Pie with Sweet Potato
- Chili Mac
- Beef Stroganoff

Classic Meatloaf

Ingredients:

- 1 lb ground beef
- 1/2 lb ground pork
- 1 medium onion, chopped
- 2 cloves garlic, minced
- 1 cup breadcrumbs
- 1/4 cup milk
- 1 egg
- 1 tbsp Worcestershire sauce
- 1 tbsp ketchup
- Salt and pepper, to taste
- 1/4 cup ketchup (for topping)

Instructions:

1. Preheat the oven to 350°F (175°C).
2. In a large bowl, combine the ground beef, ground pork, onion, garlic, breadcrumbs, milk, egg, Worcestershire sauce, ketchup, salt, and pepper.
3. Mix until well combined, then transfer the mixture to a greased loaf pan.
4. Spread a thin layer of ketchup over the top of the meatloaf.
5. Bake for 1 hour, or until the meatloaf reaches an internal temperature of 160°F (70°C).
6. Let the meatloaf rest for 10 minutes before slicing and serving.

Chicken and Dumplings

Ingredients:

- 2 tbsp butter
- 1 onion, chopped
- 2 carrots, chopped
- 2 celery stalks, chopped
- 2 cloves garlic, minced
- 6 cups chicken broth
- 2 cups cooked, shredded chicken
- 1 tsp dried thyme
- Salt and pepper, to taste
- 2 cups all-purpose flour
- 2 tsp baking powder
- 1/2 tsp salt
- 1/2 cup milk
- 1/4 cup butter, melted
- 1/4 cup chopped parsley

Instructions:

1. In a large pot, melt butter over medium heat. Add the onion, carrots, celery, and garlic, cooking for 5 minutes.
2. Add the chicken broth, shredded chicken, thyme, salt, and pepper, and bring to a boil.
3. In a separate bowl, whisk together the flour, baking powder, and salt. Add the milk and melted butter, stirring until a dough forms.

4. Drop spoonfuls of the dumpling dough into the boiling broth. Cover and simmer for 15-20 minutes, until the dumplings are cooked through.

5. Stir in chopped parsley and serve hot.

Beef Stew

Ingredients:

- 2 tbsp olive oil
- 2 lbs beef chuck, cut into cubes
- Salt and pepper, to taste
- 1 onion, chopped
- 2 carrots, peeled and chopped
- 2 celery stalks, chopped
- 4 cloves garlic, minced
- 1 cup red wine
- 4 cups beef broth
- 2 bay leaves
- 1 tsp dried thyme
- 1 lb potatoes, peeled and cubed
- 1 cup frozen peas

Instructions:

1. Heat olive oil in a large pot over medium heat. Season the beef with salt and pepper, then brown in batches, removing the beef and setting aside.

2. In the same pot, sauté the onion, carrots, celery, and garlic until softened, about 5 minutes.

3. Add the wine to deglaze the pot, scraping up any browned bits. Add the beef broth, bay leaves, thyme, and browned beef.

4. Bring to a boil, then reduce the heat and simmer for 1 hour.

5. Add the potatoes and cook for an additional 30 minutes, until the potatoes are tender.

6. Stir in the peas and cook for 5 more minutes. Serve hot.

Spaghetti and Meatballs

Ingredients:
For the meatballs:

- 1 lb ground beef
- 1/4 cup breadcrumbs
- 1/4 cup grated Parmesan
- 1 egg
- 2 cloves garlic, minced
- 1 tbsp dried oregano
- Salt and pepper, to taste
- 2 tbsp olive oil

For the sauce:

- 2 tbsp olive oil
- 1 onion, chopped
- 2 cloves garlic, minced
- 1 can (28 oz) crushed tomatoes
- 1 tsp dried basil
- 1 tsp dried oregano
- Salt and pepper, to taste
- 1 lb spaghetti

Instructions:

1. Preheat the oven to 400°F (200°C).

2. In a bowl, combine the ground beef, breadcrumbs, Parmesan, egg, garlic, oregano, salt, and pepper. Shape the mixture into meatballs.

3. Heat olive oil in a skillet over medium heat and brown the meatballs on all sides. Transfer the meatballs to a baking sheet and bake for 15-20 minutes, until cooked through.

4. In a large pot, heat olive oil over medium heat and sauté the onion and garlic for 5 minutes.

5. Add the crushed tomatoes, basil, oregano, salt, and pepper. Bring to a simmer and cook for 15 minutes.

6. Add the meatballs to the sauce and simmer for another 10 minutes.

7. Cook the spaghetti according to package instructions, then serve with the meatballs and sauce.

Macaroni and Cheese

Ingredients:

- 1 lb elbow macaroni
- 2 tbsp butter
- 2 tbsp all-purpose flour
- 2 cups whole milk
- 2 cups shredded cheddar cheese
- Salt and pepper, to taste
- 1/2 tsp mustard powder (optional)

Instructions:

1. Cook the macaroni according to package instructions, then drain and set aside.
2. In a large pot, melt the butter over medium heat. Stir in the flour and cook for 1-2 minutes.
3. Slowly add the milk, whisking constantly until smooth. Bring to a simmer and cook until the sauce thickens.
4. Stir in the cheddar cheese, salt, pepper, and mustard powder, if using, until the cheese is melted and the sauce is smooth.
5. Add the cooked macaroni to the sauce and stir to coat. Serve hot.

Chicken Pot Pie

Ingredients:

- 2 cups cooked, shredded chicken
- 2 cups frozen peas and carrots
- 1/4 cup butter
- 1/4 cup flour
- 2 cups chicken broth
- 1 cup milk
- Salt and pepper, to taste
- 1 package refrigerated pie crusts

Instructions:

1. Preheat the oven to 425°F (220°C).
2. In a large skillet, melt butter over medium heat. Stir in the flour and cook for 1-2 minutes.
3. Gradually add the chicken broth and milk, stirring until the sauce thickens.
4. Stir in the shredded chicken and frozen peas and carrots. Season with salt and pepper.
5. Roll out one pie crust and fit it into a 9-inch pie pan. Pour the chicken mixture into the crust.
6. Cover with the second pie crust and crimp the edges to seal.
7. Cut a few slits in the top crust to allow steam to escape.
8. Bake for 30-35 minutes, until the crust is golden brown. Let cool for a few minutes before serving.

Roast Chicken with Potatoes

Ingredients:

- 1 whole chicken (about 4 lbs)
- 2 tbsp olive oil
- Salt and pepper, to taste
- 1 lemon, quartered
- 4 garlic cloves, smashed
- 1 onion, quartered
- 1 lb baby potatoes, halved
- 2 tbsp fresh rosemary, chopped

Instructions:

1. Preheat the oven to 425°F (220°C).
2. Rub the chicken with olive oil, salt, and pepper. Stuff the cavity with lemon, garlic, and onion.
3. Place the chicken in a roasting pan and arrange the potatoes around it.
4. Sprinkle rosemary over the potatoes and chicken.
5. Roast for 1 hour 15 minutes, or until the chicken reaches an internal temperature of 165°F (74°C).
6. Let the chicken rest for 10 minutes before carving and serving with the potatoes.

Baked Ziti

Ingredients:

- 1 lb ziti pasta
- 1 jar (24 oz) marinara sauce
- 2 cups ricotta cheese
- 2 cups shredded mozzarella cheese
- 1/2 cup grated Parmesan cheese
- 1/4 cup fresh basil, chopped
- Salt and pepper, to taste

Instructions:

1. Preheat the oven to 375°F (190°C).
2. Cook the ziti pasta according to package instructions, then drain.
3. In a large bowl, mix the pasta with marinara sauce, ricotta cheese, 1 cup mozzarella, Parmesan cheese, basil, salt, and pepper.
4. Transfer the mixture to a baking dish and top with the remaining mozzarella.
5. Bake for 20-25 minutes, until the cheese is melted and bubbly. Serve hot.

Shepherd's Pie

Ingredients:

- 1 lb ground lamb or beef
- 1 onion, chopped
- 2 carrots, chopped
- 1 cup frozen peas
- 2 tbsp tomato paste
- 1 cup beef broth
- 2 tbsp Worcestershire sauce
- 4 cups mashed potatoes (prepared ahead of time)
- Salt and pepper, to taste

Instructions:

1. Preheat the oven to 400°F (200°C).
2. In a large skillet, brown the ground meat. Add the onion, carrots, and peas, cooking until softened.
3. Stir in the tomato paste, beef broth, Worcestershire sauce, salt, and pepper. Simmer for 10 minutes.
4. Transfer the meat mixture to a baking dish and spread the mashed potatoes over the top.
5. Bake for 20-25 minutes, until the top is golden brown.
6. Serve hot.

Sloppy Joes

Ingredients:

- 1 lb ground beef
- 1 onion, chopped
- 1 bell pepper, chopped
- 2 cloves garlic, minced
- 1 cup ketchup
- 1 tbsp Worcestershire sauce
- 1 tbsp mustard
- 1 tbsp brown sugar
- Salt and pepper, to taste
- 4 hamburger buns

Instructions:

1. In a large skillet, brown the ground beef.
2. Add the onion, bell pepper, and garlic, cooking until softened.
3. Stir in the ketchup, Worcestershire sauce, mustard, brown sugar, salt, and pepper. Simmer for 10 minutes.
4. Serve the sloppy joe mixture on hamburger buns.

Grilled Cheese and Tomato Soup

Ingredients:
For the grilled cheese:

- 8 slices bread
- 4 tbsp butter
- 8 slices cheddar cheese

For the tomato soup:

- 2 tbsp olive oil
- 1 onion, chopped
- 2 cloves garlic, minced
- 1 can (28 oz) crushed tomatoes
- 2 cups chicken broth
- Salt and pepper, to taste
- 1 tsp dried basil
- 1/2 cup heavy cream

Instructions:

1. For the soup, heat olive oil in a pot over medium heat. Add the onion and garlic, cooking until softened.
2. Add the crushed tomatoes, chicken broth, salt, pepper, and basil. Simmer for 20 minutes.
3. Blend the soup until smooth, then stir in the heavy cream.
4. For the grilled cheese, butter the bread and place cheese between two slices.

5. Grill the sandwiches in a skillet over medium heat until golden brown on both sides and the cheese is melted.

6. Serve the grilled cheese with tomato soup.

Chicken Alfredo

Ingredients:

- 1 lb fettuccine pasta
- 2 tbsp olive oil
- 2 chicken breasts, sliced
- Salt and pepper, to taste
- 4 cloves garlic, minced
- 1 cup heavy cream
- 1 cup grated Parmesan cheese
- 1/2 cup grated mozzarella cheese
- 2 tbsp butter
- Fresh parsley, chopped (for garnish)

Instructions:

1. Cook the fettuccine pasta according to the package instructions, then drain and set aside.
2. Heat olive oil in a skillet over medium heat. Season the chicken with salt and pepper, then cook until browned and cooked through, about 7-10 minutes. Remove the chicken from the skillet and set aside.
3. In the same skillet, sauté garlic in butter until fragrant, about 1 minute.
4. Add the heavy cream and bring to a simmer. Stir in the Parmesan and mozzarella cheeses, and cook until the sauce thickens, about 5 minutes.
5. Add the cooked chicken and pasta to the sauce, tossing to coat.
6. Serve with a sprinkle of chopped parsley.

Pulled Pork Sandwiches

Ingredients:

- 3 lbs pork shoulder
- 1 onion, sliced
- 2 cups BBQ sauce
- 1/4 cup apple cider vinegar
- 1/4 cup brown sugar
- 1 tbsp paprika
- 1 tbsp garlic powder
- 1 tbsp onion powder
- Salt and pepper, to taste
- 6 hamburger buns

Instructions:

1. Preheat your oven to 300°F (150°C).
2. Season the pork shoulder with paprika, garlic powder, onion powder, salt, and pepper.
3. In a roasting pan, place the sliced onion and pork shoulder. Pour the apple cider vinegar and brown sugar over the pork. Cover the pan with foil and bake for 4-5 hours, until the pork is tender and easily shreds.
4. Remove the pork from the oven and shred it with two forks.
5. Toss the shredded pork with BBQ sauce.
6. Serve the pulled pork on hamburger buns.

Beef Chili

Ingredients:

- 1 lb ground beef
- 1 onion, chopped
- 1 bell pepper, chopped
- 2 cloves garlic, minced
- 1 can (14 oz) diced tomatoes
- 1 can (15 oz) kidney beans, drained
- 1 can (15 oz) black beans, drained
- 2 tbsp chili powder
- 1 tsp cumin
- 1/2 tsp paprika
- Salt and pepper, to taste
- 1 cup beef broth

Instructions:

1. In a large pot, cook the ground beef over medium heat until browned, breaking it up into crumbles as it cooks.
2. Add the onion, bell pepper, and garlic, and cook for 5 minutes until softened.
3. Stir in the diced tomatoes, kidney beans, black beans, chili powder, cumin, paprika, salt, pepper, and beef broth.
4. Bring the chili to a simmer and cook for 30 minutes, stirring occasionally.
5. Serve hot with your choice of toppings (cheese, sour cream, etc.).

Tuna Casserole

Ingredients:

- 2 cans (5 oz each) tuna in oil, drained
- 2 cups cooked egg noodles
- 1 can (10.5 oz) cream of mushroom soup
- 1 cup frozen peas
- 1/2 cup grated cheddar cheese
- 1/2 cup breadcrumbs
- 1 tbsp butter
- Salt and pepper, to taste

Instructions:

1. Preheat the oven to 350°F (175°C).
2. In a large bowl, combine the tuna, cooked noodles, cream of mushroom soup, frozen peas, and cheddar cheese.
3. Season with salt and pepper, then mix until well combined.
4. Transfer the mixture to a greased baking dish.
5. In a small bowl, melt the butter and toss the breadcrumbs in the butter. Sprinkle the breadcrumbs over the casserole.
6. Bake for 25-30 minutes, until the top is golden brown and bubbly.

Baked Ham with Brown Sugar Glaze

Ingredients:

- 1 (6-8 lb) ham, bone-in
- 1/2 cup brown sugar
- 1/4 cup Dijon mustard
- 1/4 cup honey
- 1/4 cup apple cider vinegar
- 1/2 tsp ground cinnamon
- 1/4 tsp ground cloves

Instructions:

1. Preheat the oven to 325°F (165°C).
2. Place the ham in a roasting pan and score the surface with a sharp knife in a diamond pattern.
3. In a bowl, combine the brown sugar, mustard, honey, vinegar, cinnamon, and cloves. Stir until the sugar is dissolved.
4. Brush the glaze over the ham, reserving some glaze for later.
5. Bake the ham for 1.5-2 hours, basting every 30 minutes with the glaze.
6. Once the ham reaches an internal temperature of 140°F (60°C), remove it from the oven. Let it rest for 10 minutes before slicing and serving.

Sweet and Sour Meatballs

Ingredients:

- 1 lb ground beef
- 1/4 cup breadcrumbs
- 1/4 cup milk
- 1 egg
- Salt and pepper, to taste
- 1/4 cup vegetable oil (for frying)

For the sauce:

- 1/2 cup ketchup
- 1/4 cup vinegar
- 1/4 cup brown sugar
- 2 tbsp soy sauce
- 1/2 cup pineapple juice
- 1 tbsp cornstarch

Instructions:

1. In a bowl, mix the ground beef, breadcrumbs, milk, egg, salt, and pepper. Form into meatballs.

2. Heat oil in a large skillet over medium heat. Fry the meatballs until browned and cooked through, about 10-12 minutes.

3. In a separate saucepan, combine the ketchup, vinegar, brown sugar, soy sauce, and pineapple juice. Bring to a simmer.

4. In a small bowl, mix the cornstarch with 2 tbsp of water to make a slurry, then add to the sauce. Stir and simmer until the sauce thickens.

5. Toss the cooked meatballs in the sweet and sour sauce. Serve hot.

Chicken Fried Steak

Ingredients:

- 4 beef steaks (round or sirloin)
- 1 cup flour
- 1 tsp paprika
- 1 tsp garlic powder
- Salt and pepper, to taste
- 2 eggs, beaten
- 2 cups buttermilk
- 2 cups vegetable oil (for frying)
- Gravy (store-bought or homemade)

Instructions:

1. Preheat the oil in a large skillet over medium heat.
2. Season the steaks with salt and pepper.
3. In a bowl, combine the flour, paprika, garlic powder, salt, and pepper.
4. Dip each steak in the buttermilk, then dredge in the flour mixture, coating both sides.
5. Fry the steaks for 4-5 minutes per side, until golden brown and crispy.
6. Drain the steaks on paper towels, then serve with gravy.

Stir-Fried Vegetables with Rice

Ingredients:

- 1 tbsp vegetable oil
- 1 onion, chopped
- 2 cloves garlic, minced
- 1 bell pepper, chopped
- 1 carrot, julienned
- 1 zucchini, sliced
- 1 cup cooked rice
- 2 tbsp soy sauce
- 1 tbsp sesame oil
- 1 tbsp rice vinegar
- Salt and pepper, to taste
- 1 tbsp sesame seeds (optional)

Instructions:

1. Heat the vegetable oil in a large skillet or wok over medium-high heat.
2. Add the onion and garlic and sauté for 2 minutes.
3. Add the bell pepper, carrot, and zucchini, and stir-fry for another 5-7 minutes, until the vegetables are tender-crisp.
4. Add the cooked rice, soy sauce, sesame oil, and rice vinegar, stirring to combine.
5. Season with salt and pepper, then serve with sesame seeds, if desired.

Meatball Sub

Ingredients:

- 1 batch meatballs (prepared from the previous recipe)
- 4 sub rolls
- 1 cup marinara sauce
- 1 cup shredded mozzarella cheese

Instructions:

1. Preheat the oven to 375°F (190°C).
2. Heat the marinara sauce in a saucepan and add the cooked meatballs.
3. Split the sub rolls and place the meatballs and sauce inside.
4. Top with mozzarella cheese.
5. Bake for 10-12 minutes, until the cheese is melted and bubbly.

Chicken Parmesan

Ingredients:

- 4 chicken breasts
- 1 cup breadcrumbs
- 1/2 cup grated Parmesan cheese
- 1 egg, beaten
- 2 cups marinara sauce
- 1 1/2 cups shredded mozzarella cheese
- Salt and pepper, to taste
- Olive oil (for frying)

Instructions:

1. Preheat the oven to 375°F (190°C).
2. Season the chicken breasts with salt and pepper.
3. In a shallow bowl, mix the breadcrumbs and Parmesan cheese. Dip each chicken breast in the egg, then coat in the breadcrumb mixture.
4. Heat olive oil in a skillet over medium heat and fry the chicken until golden brown on both sides, about 4 minutes per side.
5. Transfer the chicken to a baking dish, top with marinara sauce and mozzarella cheese.
6. Bake for 20 minutes, until the chicken is cooked through and the cheese is melted.

Beef Tacos

Ingredients:

- 1 lb ground beef
- 1 onion, chopped
- 2 cloves garlic, minced
- 1 packet taco seasoning
- 1/2 cup water
- 8 taco shells or tortillas
- Toppings: lettuce, cheese, sour cream, salsa, avocado, cilantro, etc.

Instructions:

1. In a large skillet, cook the ground beef over medium heat until browned. Drain any excess fat.
2. Add the chopped onion and minced garlic, and cook for another 3 minutes until softened.
3. Stir in the taco seasoning and water, and simmer for 5-7 minutes, until the sauce thickens.
4. Warm the taco shells or tortillas according to package instructions.
5. Fill the taco shells with the beef mixture and your favorite toppings. Serve immediately.

Homemade Pizza

Ingredients for dough:

- 2 1/4 tsp active dry yeast
- 1 1/2 cups warm water
- 1 tbsp sugar
- 3 1/2 cups all-purpose flour
- 2 tbsp olive oil
- 1 tsp salt

Ingredients for toppings:

- 1/2 cup pizza sauce
- 1 1/2 cups shredded mozzarella cheese
- Toppings of your choice (pepperoni, mushrooms, bell peppers, etc.)

Instructions:

1. In a small bowl, dissolve the yeast and sugar in warm water. Let sit for 5-10 minutes, until frothy.

2. In a large bowl, combine the flour and salt. Add the yeast mixture and olive oil. Mix until a dough forms.

3. Knead the dough on a floured surface for 5-7 minutes, until smooth. Place it in a lightly oiled bowl, cover, and let rise for 1-2 hours.

4. Preheat your oven to 475°F (245°C).

5. Punch down the dough and divide it into two portions. Roll out each portion into a circle on a floured surface.

6. Spread a thin layer of pizza sauce on each dough circle. Sprinkle with mozzarella cheese and add your preferred toppings.

7. Bake on a pizza stone or baking sheet for 10-12 minutes, until the crust is golden and the cheese is bubbly.

Eggplant Parmesan

Ingredients:

- 2 medium eggplants, sliced into 1/2-inch rounds
- 2 eggs, beaten
- 2 cups breadcrumbs
- 1 cup grated Parmesan cheese
- 2 cups marinara sauce
- 2 cups shredded mozzarella cheese
- Olive oil (for frying)
- Fresh basil, chopped (optional)

Instructions:

1. Preheat the oven to 375°F (190°C).
2. Dip each eggplant slice into the beaten eggs, then coat with the breadcrumb and Parmesan mixture.
3. Heat olive oil in a skillet over medium heat. Fry the eggplant slices until golden brown on both sides, about 2-3 minutes per side.
4. In a baking dish, spread a thin layer of marinara sauce. Layer the fried eggplant slices over the sauce.
5. Top each layer with mozzarella cheese and marinara sauce.
6. Bake for 20 minutes, until the cheese is melted and bubbly. Garnish with fresh basil before serving.

Fried Chicken

Ingredients:

- 4 chicken pieces (drumsticks, thighs, or breasts)
- 1 1/2 cups buttermilk
- 1 tbsp hot sauce (optional)
- 2 cups all-purpose flour
- 1 tbsp paprika
- 1 tsp garlic powder
- Salt and pepper, to taste
- Vegetable oil (for frying)

Instructions:

1. In a bowl, combine the buttermilk and hot sauce. Place the chicken pieces in the mixture and marinate for at least 1 hour (or overnight in the fridge).
2. In a shallow bowl, combine the flour, paprika, garlic powder, salt, and pepper.
3. Heat vegetable oil in a large skillet over medium heat.
4. Dredge each piece of chicken in the seasoned flour, pressing down to coat well.
5. Fry the chicken in batches, cooking each piece for 10-12 minutes, until golden brown and cooked through (internal temperature should reach 165°F/74°C).
6. Drain on paper towels and serve hot.

BBQ Ribs

Ingredients:

- 2 racks of baby back ribs
- Salt and pepper, to taste
- 1 cup BBQ sauce (store-bought or homemade)

Instructions:

1. Preheat your oven to 300°F (150°C).
2. Remove the silver skin from the back of the ribs. Season both sides of the ribs with salt and pepper.
3. Wrap the ribs in aluminum foil and bake in the oven for 2.5-3 hours.
4. Preheat a grill or grill pan over medium-high heat.
5. Remove the ribs from the foil and brush with BBQ sauce.
6. Grill the ribs for 5-10 minutes, turning and brushing with more sauce, until the ribs are caramelized and have grill marks.
7. Slice and serve with additional BBQ sauce.

Beef and Broccoli Stir Fry

Ingredients:

- 1 lb flank steak, thinly sliced
- 2 cups broccoli florets
- 2 tbsp soy sauce
- 2 tbsp oyster sauce
- 1 tbsp hoisin sauce
- 1 tsp sesame oil
- 2 cloves garlic, minced
- 1 tbsp vegetable oil (for stir-frying)
- 1 tsp cornstarch mixed with 1 tbsp water (optional, for thickening)

Instructions:

1. Heat vegetable oil in a wok or large skillet over high heat. Add the sliced beef and stir-fry for 3-4 minutes until browned.
2. Add the broccoli florets and cook for another 2 minutes.
3. In a small bowl, mix the soy sauce, oyster sauce, hoisin sauce, sesame oil, and garlic. Pour the sauce over the beef and broccoli, and cook for 2 more minutes.
4. If you prefer a thicker sauce, add the cornstarch slurry and stir until the sauce thickens.
5. Serve hot with steamed rice.

Spaghetti Carbonara

Ingredients:

- 1 lb spaghetti
- 4 oz pancetta or bacon, diced
- 3 large eggs
- 1 cup grated Parmesan cheese
- 1/2 cup heavy cream (optional)
- Salt and pepper, to taste
- Fresh parsley, chopped (for garnish)

Instructions:

1. Cook the spaghetti according to package instructions, reserving 1 cup of pasta water before draining.
2. While the pasta cooks, fry the pancetta or bacon in a large skillet over medium heat until crispy.
3. In a bowl, whisk together the eggs, Parmesan, and heavy cream (if using). Season with salt and pepper.
4. Toss the cooked spaghetti with the bacon and rendered fat.
5. Slowly pour the egg mixture into the pasta, stirring constantly to create a creamy sauce. Add pasta water as needed to achieve your desired consistency.
6. Garnish with fresh parsley and serve immediately.

Shrimp Scampi

Ingredients:

- 1 lb large shrimp, peeled and deveined
- 8 oz spaghetti or linguine
- 4 cloves garlic, minced
- 1/4 cup butter
- 1/4 cup olive oil
- 1/2 cup white wine
- 1 tbsp lemon juice
- Salt and pepper, to taste
- Fresh parsley, chopped (for garnish)

Instructions:

1. Cook the pasta according to package instructions. Drain and set aside.
2. In a large skillet, melt the butter and olive oil over medium heat. Add the garlic and sauté for 1 minute until fragrant.
3. Add the shrimp and cook until pink, about 3-4 minutes.
4. Add the white wine and lemon juice, and simmer for 2 minutes.
5. Toss the cooked pasta into the skillet and stir to coat in the sauce.
6. Season with salt and pepper, garnish with parsley, and serve hot.

Grilled Hamburgers

Ingredients:

- 1 lb ground beef (80% lean)
- Salt and pepper, to taste
- 4 hamburger buns
- Toppings: lettuce, tomato, cheese, pickles, etc.

Instructions:

1. Preheat the grill to medium-high heat.
2. Season the ground beef with salt and pepper, then form into 4 patties.
3. Grill the patties for 4-5 minutes per side, until the desired doneness is reached.
4. Toast the hamburger buns on the grill for 1-2 minutes.
5. Assemble the burgers with your favorite toppings and serve immediately.

Potato Salad

Ingredients:

- 2 lbs potatoes, peeled and cut into chunks
- 1/2 cup mayonnaise
- 1/4 cup sour cream
- 1 tbsp Dijon mustard
- 1 tbsp apple cider vinegar
- Salt and pepper, to taste
- 1/2 cup chopped celery
- 1/4 cup chopped red onion
- 2 boiled eggs, chopped (optional)

Instructions:

1. Boil the potatoes in salted water for 10-12 minutes until tender. Drain and let cool.
2. In a large bowl, combine the mayonnaise, sour cream, mustard, and vinegar.
3. Add the cooled potatoes, celery, red onion, and boiled eggs (if using). Stir to combine.
4. Season with salt and pepper to taste. Chill for 1 hour before serving.

Biscuits and Gravy

Ingredients for Biscuits:

- 2 cups all-purpose flour
- 1 tbsp baking powder
- 1 tsp salt
- 1/4 cup unsalted butter, cold and cubed
- 3/4 cup buttermilk

Ingredients for Gravy:

- 1 lb breakfast sausage
- 1/4 cup all-purpose flour
- 2 cups milk
- Salt and pepper, to taste

Instructions:

1. Preheat the oven to 425°F (220°C).
2. In a large bowl, combine flour, baking powder, and salt. Add the cubed butter and use a pastry cutter or fork to cut the butter into the flour until it resembles coarse crumbs.
3. Pour in the buttermilk and stir until just combined.
4. Turn the dough onto a floured surface and gently knead 4-5 times. Roll it out to about 1-inch thick, then cut into rounds.
5. Place the biscuits on a baking sheet and bake for 12-15 minutes until golden brown.
6. For the gravy, cook the sausage in a skillet over medium heat until browned. Remove the sausage and set aside, reserving some of the drippings in the pan.

7. Stir in flour and cook for 1-2 minutes to make a roux. Gradually add the milk, stirring constantly to prevent lumps.

8. Bring to a simmer and cook until thickened. Season with salt and pepper.

9. Serve the biscuits with the sausage gravy poured over the top.

Fettuccine Alfredo

Ingredients:

- 12 oz fettuccine pasta
- 1/2 cup unsalted butter
- 1 cup heavy cream
- 1 1/2 cups grated Parmesan cheese
- 2 cloves garlic, minced
- Salt and pepper, to taste
- Fresh parsley, chopped (for garnish)

Instructions:

1. Cook the fettuccine pasta according to package instructions. Drain and set aside.
2. In a large skillet, melt the butter over medium heat. Add the garlic and cook for 1 minute until fragrant.
3. Pour in the heavy cream and bring to a simmer. Cook for 3-4 minutes until the cream has thickened slightly.
4. Stir in the Parmesan cheese and cook until the sauce is smooth and creamy.
5. Toss the cooked fettuccine into the sauce and stir to coat.
6. Season with salt and pepper, and garnish with fresh parsley. Serve immediately.

Stuffed Bell Peppers

Ingredients:

- 4 bell peppers, tops cut off and seeds removed
- 1 lb ground beef or turkey
- 1 cup cooked rice
- 1 can diced tomatoes (14.5 oz)
- 1 small onion, chopped
- 1 cup shredded cheese (cheddar or mozzarella)
- 1 tsp garlic powder
- 1 tsp dried oregano
- Salt and pepper, to taste

Instructions:

1. Preheat the oven to 375°F (190°C).
2. In a skillet, cook the ground meat and chopped onion over medium heat until browned and cooked through. Drain any excess fat.
3. Stir in the cooked rice, diced tomatoes, garlic powder, oregano, salt, and pepper.
4. Stuff the bell peppers with the meat and rice mixture and place them in a baking dish.
5. Top each pepper with shredded cheese.
6. Cover the baking dish with foil and bake for 30-35 minutes.
7. Remove the foil and bake for an additional 5-10 minutes until the cheese is melted and bubbly.

Chicken Fajitas

Ingredients:

- 1 lb chicken breast, thinly sliced
- 1 onion, sliced
- 1 bell pepper, sliced
- 2 tbsp olive oil
- 1 tsp chili powder
- 1 tsp cumin
- 1/2 tsp paprika
- 1/2 tsp garlic powder
- Salt and pepper, to taste
- 8 small flour tortillas
- Toppings: sour cream, guacamole, salsa, cilantro, lime wedges

Instructions:

1. In a large skillet, heat the olive oil over medium-high heat.
2. Season the chicken with chili powder, cumin, paprika, garlic powder, salt, and pepper.
3. Cook the chicken in the skillet until browned and cooked through, about 5-7 minutes. Remove the chicken and set aside.
4. In the same skillet, add the sliced onion and bell pepper. Cook for 3-4 minutes until softened.
5. Return the chicken to the skillet and toss everything together.
6. Warm the tortillas in the microwave or on a dry skillet.
7. Serve the fajita mixture in the tortillas with your favorite toppings.

Grilled Salmon

Ingredients:

- 4 salmon fillets
- 2 tbsp olive oil
- 1 tbsp lemon juice
- 1 tsp garlic powder
- 1 tsp dried thyme
- Salt and pepper, to taste

Instructions:

1. Preheat your grill to medium-high heat.
2. Brush the salmon fillets with olive oil and drizzle with lemon juice.
3. Sprinkle with garlic powder, thyme, salt, and pepper.
4. Grill the salmon for 4-5 minutes per side, or until cooked through and the flesh flakes easily with a fork.
5. Serve with additional lemon wedges and your choice of sides.

Beef Burritos

Ingredients:

- 1 lb ground beef
- 1 packet taco seasoning
- 1/4 cup water
- 8 flour tortillas
- 1 can refried beans
- 1 cup shredded cheese
- 1/2 cup sour cream
- Salsa, for serving

Instructions:

1. In a skillet, cook the ground beef over medium heat until browned. Drain any excess fat.
2. Stir in the taco seasoning and water, and simmer for 5-7 minutes until thickened.
3. Warm the tortillas in the microwave or on a skillet.
4. Spread a layer of refried beans on each tortilla, then add the beef mixture.
5. Top with shredded cheese, sour cream, and salsa.
6. Roll up the tortillas, folding in the sides to secure the filling.
7. Serve immediately.

Tacos al Pastor

Ingredients:

- 1 lb pork shoulder, thinly sliced
- 1/2 cup pineapple, chopped
- 1/4 cup onion, chopped
- 2 cloves garlic, minced
- 2 tbsp adobo sauce (from chipotle peppers)
- 1 tsp cumin
- 1 tsp paprika
- 1 tbsp lime juice
- 8 small corn tortillas
- Toppings: cilantro, diced onion, lime wedges

Instructions:

1. In a bowl, combine the pork, pineapple, onion, garlic, adobo sauce, cumin, paprika, and lime juice. Marinate for at least 1 hour (or overnight).
2. Heat a skillet over medium-high heat. Cook the marinated pork mixture for 5-7 minutes until browned and cooked through.
3. Warm the tortillas in the skillet or microwave.
4. Serve the pork mixture in the tortillas with fresh cilantro, diced onion, and lime wedges.

Chicken Quesadillas

Ingredients:

- 2 chicken breasts, cooked and shredded
- 1 cup shredded cheese (cheddar, mozzarella, or a blend)
- 1/2 cup salsa
- 4 flour tortillas
- 2 tbsp olive oil

Instructions:

1. In a bowl, combine the shredded chicken, cheese, and salsa.
2. Heat 1 tbsp olive oil in a skillet over medium heat.
3. Place one tortilla in the skillet, and spread a thin layer of the chicken mixture on top.
4. Place another tortilla on top and cook for 2-3 minutes until golden brown.
5. Flip the quesadilla and cook for another 2-3 minutes until the cheese is melted.
6. Remove from the skillet, slice into wedges, and serve with sour cream and salsa.

Fish Tacos

Ingredients:

- 1 lb white fish fillets (such as cod or tilapia)
- 1 tsp chili powder
- 1 tsp cumin
- 1/2 tsp paprika
- Salt and pepper, to taste
- 8 small corn tortillas
- 1/2 cup shredded cabbage
- 1/4 cup sour cream
- 1 tbsp lime juice
- Salsa, for serving

Instructions:

1. Preheat your grill or skillet to medium-high heat.
2. Season the fish fillets with chili powder, cumin, paprika, salt, and pepper.
3. Grill or cook the fish for 3-4 minutes per side until cooked through and flakes easily with a fork.
4. Warm the tortillas and fill with the grilled fish.
5. Top with shredded cabbage, a drizzle of sour cream mixed with lime juice, and salsa.
6. Serve with lime wedges.

Meatloaf Sandwich

Ingredients:

- 2 slices of meatloaf (from a previously made meatloaf)
- 2 slices of bread (white, whole wheat, or a roll)
- 1 tbsp mayonnaise or mustard
- Lettuce, tomato, and pickles for garnish

Instructions:

1. Toast the bread slices lightly in a toaster or on a skillet.
2. Spread mayonnaise or mustard on one slice of bread.
3. Place the slices of meatloaf on top of the bread, and add lettuce, tomato, and pickles.
4. Top with the other slice of bread, cut in half, and serve.

Clam Chowder

Ingredients:

- 2 tbsp butter
- 1 onion, finely chopped
- 2 celery stalks, chopped
- 2 cloves garlic, minced
- 4 cups chicken broth
- 4 cups potatoes, peeled and diced
- 2 cups heavy cream
- 1 can (6.5 oz) clams, drained (reserve the liquid)
- 1 tsp thyme
- Salt and pepper, to taste
- 1/4 cup fresh parsley, chopped (for garnish)
- 1/2 cup cooked bacon, crumbled (optional)

Instructions:

1. In a large pot, melt the butter over medium heat. Add the onion, celery, and garlic. Cook until softened, about 5 minutes.

2. Add the chicken broth and potatoes. Bring to a boil, then reduce the heat and simmer for 10-15 minutes, until the potatoes are tender.

3. Stir in the heavy cream and reserved clam liquid. Bring the mixture back to a simmer and cook for another 5 minutes.

4. Add the clams, thyme, salt, and pepper, and cook for 2-3 more minutes.

5. Garnish with parsley and crumbled bacon, if desired, and serve hot.

Roasted Vegetable Soup

Ingredients:

- 2 cups carrots, peeled and chopped
- 2 cups zucchini, chopped
- 1 red bell pepper, chopped
- 1 onion, chopped
- 3 cloves garlic, minced
- 1 tbsp olive oil
- 4 cups vegetable broth
- 1 tsp thyme
- 1 tsp cumin
- Salt and pepper, to taste
- Fresh parsley, chopped (for garnish)

Instructions:

1. Preheat the oven to 400°F (200°C).
2. Toss the carrots, zucchini, bell pepper, and onion with olive oil, salt, and pepper. Spread the vegetables in a single layer on a baking sheet.
3. Roast the vegetables for 20-25 minutes, stirring once halfway through, until tender and caramelized.
4. In a large pot, sauté the garlic for 1-2 minutes until fragrant. Add the roasted vegetables, vegetable broth, thyme, cumin, salt, and pepper.
5. Bring to a boil, then reduce the heat and simmer for 10 minutes.
6. Use an immersion blender to blend the soup until smooth, or transfer to a blender in batches.

7. Garnish with fresh parsley and serve hot.

Pulled Chicken Tacos

Ingredients:

- 4 chicken breasts
- 1 cup chicken broth
- 1 tbsp chili powder
- 1 tsp cumin
- 1 tsp paprika
- 1 tsp garlic powder
- Salt and pepper, to taste
- 8 small tortillas
- Toppings: shredded lettuce, salsa, cheese, sour cream, cilantro

Instructions:

1. Place the chicken breasts in a slow cooker. Add the chicken broth, chili powder, cumin, paprika, garlic powder, salt, and pepper.
2. Cook on low for 6-8 hours, or on high for 3-4 hours, until the chicken is tender and easily shreds.
3. Shred the chicken using two forks.
4. Warm the tortillas and fill each with pulled chicken.
5. Top with your favorite toppings and serve immediately.

Grilled Shrimp Skewers

Ingredients:

- 1 lb shrimp, peeled and deveined
- 2 tbsp olive oil
- 2 tbsp lemon juice
- 2 garlic cloves, minced
- 1 tsp paprika
- 1 tsp cumin
- Salt and pepper, to taste
- Fresh parsley, chopped (for garnish)

Instructions:

1. In a bowl, combine olive oil, lemon juice, garlic, paprika, cumin, salt, and pepper.
2. Toss the shrimp in the marinade and let sit for 15-20 minutes.
3. Preheat the grill to medium-high heat.
4. Thread the shrimp onto skewers.
5. Grill the shrimp for 2-3 minutes per side until pink and cooked through.
6. Garnish with fresh parsley and serve hot.

Caesar Salad with Grilled Chicken

Ingredients:

- 2 boneless, skinless chicken breasts
- 4 cups romaine lettuce, chopped
- 1/4 cup Caesar dressing
- 1/4 cup Parmesan cheese, grated
- Croutons, for topping
- Salt and pepper, to taste
- Olive oil, for grilling

Instructions:

1. Season the chicken breasts with salt and pepper.
2. Heat a grill or grill pan over medium heat and drizzle with olive oil.
3. Grill the chicken for 5-7 minutes per side until cooked through and juices run clear.
4. Let the chicken rest for a few minutes before slicing.
5. In a large bowl, toss the romaine lettuce with Caesar dressing and Parmesan cheese.
6. Top the salad with the sliced grilled chicken and croutons. Serve immediately.

Baked Chicken Drumsticks

Ingredients:

- 8 chicken drumsticks
- 2 tbsp olive oil
- 1 tsp garlic powder
- 1 tsp paprika
- 1 tsp onion powder
- 1/2 tsp salt
- 1/2 tsp pepper
- Fresh parsley, chopped (for garnish)

Instructions:

1. Preheat the oven to 400°F (200°C).
2. Pat the chicken drumsticks dry with paper towels.
3. In a bowl, mix olive oil, garlic powder, paprika, onion powder, salt, and pepper.
4. Rub the mixture over the drumsticks.
5. Arrange the drumsticks on a baking sheet and bake for 35-40 minutes, or until the internal temperature reaches 165°F (74°C).
6. Garnish with fresh parsley and serve.

Shepherd's Pie with Sweet Potato

Ingredients:

- 1 lb ground beef or lamb
- 1 onion, chopped
- 2 carrots, chopped
- 1 cup peas
- 2 tbsp tomato paste
- 1/4 cup beef broth
- 2 tbsp Worcestershire sauce
- 4 large sweet potatoes, peeled and cubed
- 1/4 cup milk
- 2 tbsp butter
- Salt and pepper, to taste

Instructions:

1. Preheat the oven to 375°F (190°C).
2. In a large skillet, brown the ground meat over medium heat. Add the onion and carrots, and cook for 5-7 minutes until softened.
3. Stir in the tomato paste, beef broth, Worcestershire sauce, peas, salt, and pepper. Cook for another 5 minutes.
4. In a separate pot, boil the sweet potatoes until tender, about 10-15 minutes. Drain and mash with milk and butter. Season with salt and pepper.
5. Spread the meat mixture into a baking dish. Top with the mashed sweet potatoes.
6. Bake for 20-25 minutes, or until the top is golden brown. Serve hot.

Chili Mac

Ingredients:

- 1 lb ground beef
- 1 onion, chopped
- 2 cloves garlic, minced
- 1 can (15 oz) chili beans
- 1 can (14.5 oz) diced tomatoes
- 2 tbsp chili powder
- 1 tsp cumin
- 1 cup elbow macaroni, cooked
- 2 cups shredded cheddar cheese
- Salt and pepper, to taste

Instructions:

1. In a large skillet, brown the ground beef with the onion and garlic. Drain excess fat.
2. Stir in the chili beans, diced tomatoes, chili powder, cumin, salt, and pepper. Simmer for 10 minutes.
3. Add the cooked macaroni and stir until well combined.
4. Stir in the shredded cheese and cook for an additional 2-3 minutes until the cheese is melted.
5. Serve hot.

Beef Stroganoff

Ingredients:

- 1 lb beef sirloin or tenderloin, sliced thinly
- 1 onion, chopped
- 2 cloves garlic, minced
- 2 tbsp flour
- 1 cup beef broth
- 1 cup sour cream
- 2 tbsp Dijon mustard
- 2 tbsp olive oil
- Salt and pepper, to taste
- 1/4 cup fresh parsley, chopped (for garnish)

Instructions:

1. Heat the olive oil in a large skillet over medium-high heat. Add the beef slices and cook for 3-4 minutes until browned. Remove the beef from the skillet and set aside.
2. In the same skillet, add the onion and garlic, and cook for 3 minutes until softened.
3. Stir in the flour and cook for 1 minute to form a roux.
4. Gradually add the beef broth, stirring constantly to prevent lumps. Bring to a simmer and cook for 5 minutes.
5. Stir in the sour cream, Dijon mustard, and cooked beef. Simmer for an additional 5 minutes until thickened.
6. Season with salt and pepper, and garnish with parsley before serving.

www.ingramcontent.com/pod-product-compliance
Lightning Source LLC
LaVergne TN
LVHW081319060526
838201LV00055B/2360